Steve Jobs

Apple and Beyond

By Adria F. Klein

Published in the United States of America
by the Hameray Publishing Group, Inc.

Text © Adria F. Klein
Maps © Hameray Publishing Group, Inc.
Published 2009

Publisher: Raymond Yuen
Series Editors: Adria F. Klein and Alan Trussell-Cullen
Project Editor: Kaitlyn Nichols
Designers: Lois Stanfield and Linda Lockowitz
Map Designer: Barry Age

Photo Credits: AP: cover, 1, 4, 13, 20–21
Corbis: back cover, 18, 22, 33
Getty: 16–17, 28, 31

Trademarks used in this text: *Apple 1*, *Apple II*, *Apple Computers*, *Apple Macintosh*, the *Apple* logo, *iPhone*, *iPod*, and *iTunes* are trademarks of Apple, Inc.; *Atari* and *Asteroids* are registered trademarks of Atari Interactive, Inc.; App Store is a registered service mark of Apple, Inc.

Hameray Publishing Group, Inc. disclaims any proprietary interest in trademarks and trade names other than its own.

ISBN 978-1-60559-071-4

Printed in China

1 2 3 4 5 SIP 13 12 11 10 09

Contents

Chapter 1

Who is Steve Jobs?

"Your time is limited, so don't waste it living someone else's life." That is what Steven Paul Jobs told students in a graduation speech at Stanford University in June 2005.

He wasn't just telling the new graduates how they should live their lives. He was telling them how he had lived *his* life so far. The students listened carefully. They knew this was the man who was a founder of Apple Computers—the **technology** company that

◀ Steve Jobs delivers a speech to graduates at Stanford University.

had given the world the Apple computer and many other exciting new products, including the iPod and the iPhone.

As the **CEO** or head of Apple Computers, he has helped make the company a world leader. How has he lived his own life? How did he get to where he is today? His story is a fascinating one of hard work, determination, and creativity.

> "The only way to do great work is to love what you do. If you haven't found it yet, keep looking. Don't settle. As with all matters of the heart, you'll know when you find it." —Steve Jobs

Chapter 2

Growing Up in Silicon Valley

Steve Jobs was born in San Francisco, California, on February 24, 1955. He was adopted by Justin and Clara Jobs of Mountain View, a town in northern California. They gave him the name Steven Paul.

Steve Jobs grew up at an exciting time when all kinds of new inventions were being developed. The United States was leading the way in technology. Television, telephones, computers, and other technologies were all constantly being developed and improved.

Steve Jobs was lucky for another reason, too. He was living in Northern California.

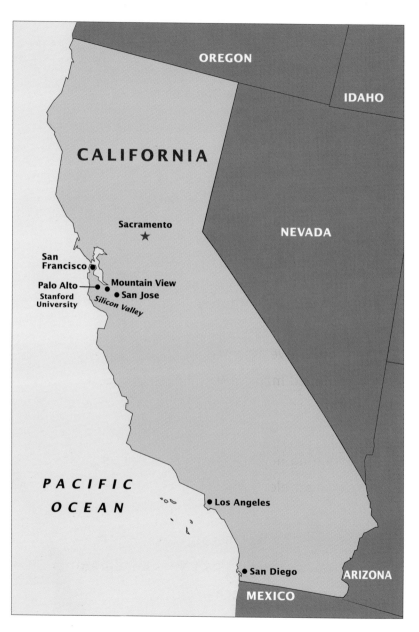

OREGON

IDAHO

CALIFORNIA

Sacramento

San
Francisco

NEVADA

Palo Alto
Stanford
University

Mountain View
San Jose
Silicon Valley

PACIFIC
OCEAN

Los Angeles

San Diego

ARIZONA

MEXICO

8

It was here that many exciting new ideas and products were being developed. Most of the new technology companies were located here and many of the young inventors who worked for them were living near Stanford University in Palo Alto.

Later this area would be nicknamed "Silicon Valley." This was because most of the products made by these technology companies used the **silicon chip** to control the way the products worked.

When Steve Jobs was in high school, he attended many after-school lectures at the Hewlett-Packard Company in Palo Alto. Hewlett-Packard is a company that led the way in inventing new computers and printers and many other electronic machines.

One summer, Jobs went to work at Hewlett-Packard. Here Jobs met Steve Wozniak, a man who would play a big part as a **collaborator** in his future work in technology.

After graduating high school in 1972, Jobs enrolled in Reed College in Portland, Oregon. He attended Reed College for only one semester. He was interested in many subjects and was always interested in studying and learning. Even after he had dropped out of college, he continued to sit in on different classes. But Jobs had plans for his future and he didn't think college would help him achieve his goals. He was heading in a different direction.

In 1974 Jobs returned to California. He met up again with Steve Wozniak, the friend he had met at his summer job at Hewlett-Packard. Jobs and Wozniak spent a lot of time thinking and talking about new uses for the computer.

Chapter 3

Exploring Many Creative Ideas

Jobs wasn't only interested in computers. He had always been interested in studying many things, including different religious beliefs and how people in other parts of the world looked at life. Jobs decided he needed to go to India to learn about the different religious beliefs there. To save enough money for the trip, he took a job at a company called Atari. Atari was one of the first companies to make video games.

When Jobs had saved enough money, he and a friend left for India. Together they backpacked around the country. Jobs said later that the simple approach to life he

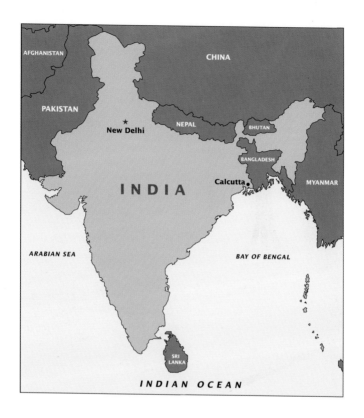

experienced in India had a big impact on the
way he thought about the world.

After some time in India, he came back to
the United States. He went to work for Atari
again. But while he was working there, he was
thinking about what he would really like to be
doing with his life.

▲ Atari made Asteroids, one of the first video games.

Chapter 4

Creator and Inventor

Jobs and Wozniak continued to work for technology companies. But in their spare time they began to work together on their own projects. They designed their first computer and built the **prototype**, or first model, in Jobs' garage. They wanted to start their own company to make and sell computers. But first, they needed some money, so they sold some of their most valuable possessions. Their work on computers quickly attracted money from **investors**, too.

They needed a name for their new company. Jobs came up with the name "Apple." Some folks say this name came from a very happy summer Jobs spent picking apples in an orchard in Oregon. Others have commented that Jobs also believed that the apple was really the perfect fruit. Whatever the real reason for the name, Jobs and Wozniak called their first computer the "Apple I" and it sold for around seven hundred dollars.

Soon, orders began coming in so fast that they needed to set up a **production line** to make their computers. Jobs encouraged Wozniak to leave his job at Hewlett-Packard so he could work for Apple. Wozniak became the vice president of the new company and was in charge of **research**. Eventually, Jobs and Wozniak managed to earn a reported three-quarters of a million dollars from the sales of the Apple I.

Up to now, computers were mainly used by businesses. But Jobs **marketed** the Apple I to people who wanted to have a computer for their own personal use. The idea of a personal computer was quickly becoming popular.

Meanwhile, Jobs and Wozniak kept working to make their computer better. In 1977, just a

▶
Steve Jobs and
Steve Wozniak at
a computer fair
in 1977.

year later, Jobs and Wozniak had their newest computer, Apple II, ready to sell.

The Apple II was a simple and very useful computer. It was fun, too—the new monitor

was available with color **computer graphics**. This computer was very popular and lots of people bought it.

Things were changing quickly in technology. In fact, to meet the growing demand for home and school computers, over sixteen thousand software programs were created for the Apple II. Jobs and Wozniak were creating

▲ Steve Jobs in his office at Apple Computers in 1981.

innovative products, but they had even more new ideas. They kept working together until 1981 when Wozniak was hurt in a plane crash and stopped working full-time at Apple.

In 1984 Jobs launched the Apple Macintosh. This new computer put all of the basic computer equipment in one unit.

It was also the first personal computer to use a mouse. This was a very popular computer and for more than twenty years Jobs has kept refining and improving it.

> *"What a computer is to me is the most remarkable tool that we have ever come up with. It's the equivalent of a bicycle for our minds"* —Steve Jobs

In 1985, due to some disagreements with others, Jobs left Apple for a time. While he was away from Apple, Jobs developed other computers and computer products. But in 1996, with a major business deal, Jobs returned to Apple to lead the company.

After returning to Apple, Jobs has led the development of many exciting new products, including the iPod and the iPhone.

The iPod is a very small music player that stores songs and music. It is hugely popular all over the world. Apple brought out the first

iPod in 2001 and added iTunes in 2003 to provide an easy way to download music.

▼ Steve Jobs introduces new iPod models in 2008.

The iPhone is one of his newest inventions.
Jobs wanted to get into the cell phone
business and worked hard to build a better

▲ Steve Jobs introduces the new iPhone.

phone. The iPhone is both a phone and a powerful mini-computer. People can use it to surf the internet, take photos, and do many more creative things. Over thirteen million iPhones sold in a very short time after it was introduced.

> *"I think we're having fun. I think our customers really like our products. And we're always trying to do better."* —Steve Jobs

Jobs has introduced many new products in his leadership at Apple and the launching of a new product is always an exciting and special event. But Steve Jobs is not only an inventor with lots of good ideas. He is also a very good businessman.

Chapter 5

Leading Apple

In the business world, Steve Jobs is considered a very successful CEO. He obviously loves his work and is very enthusiastic about everything he does. He has changed the way people think about and use computers. But he has also changed the way we listen to music and the way we use machines in our lives for both work and play.

Jobs isn't like lots of other business leaders. He is very confident and energetic and expects a lot of the people around him. He also likes to take part in everything his company is doing. People call this being "hands-on." This means he takes part in almost everything that is created and decided at Apple.

Jobs has been quoted in newspapers and magazines as saying, "We just want to make great products."

Steve Jobs holds big celebrations when he introduces a new product. Lots of people attend and everyone gets very excited about the new product. Often there are appearances by famous actors and musicians.

Chapter 6

Computers and the Movies

Jobs has always been interested in finding new uses for computers. In the 1980's he began to become interested in using computers to make **animated movies**. Before this, most animation was done using thousands of drawings or by taking lots of photographs of models or objects. By slowly changing the picture or moving the object while filming, things begin to look like they are alive or animated. But Jobs was interested in doing all this on a computer screen using computer graphics.

In 1986 Jobs bought a computer graphics company and renamed it "Pixar." The Pixar

Animation Studios began making short animated movies and commercials using computers to do all of the animation. A big break came in 1991 when Pixar teamed up with Walt Disney Studios to make full-length movies.

The first of these movies was *Toy Story* (1995). It was the world's first fully computer animated feature film and was a huge success.

> *"We believe it's the biggest advance in animation since Walt Disney started it all with the release of* Snow White *fifty years ago."*   —Steve Jobs, on *Toy Story*

Other fun family movies followed including, *A Bug's Life* (1998), *Toy Story 2* (1999), *Monsters, Inc.* (2001), *Finding Nemo*

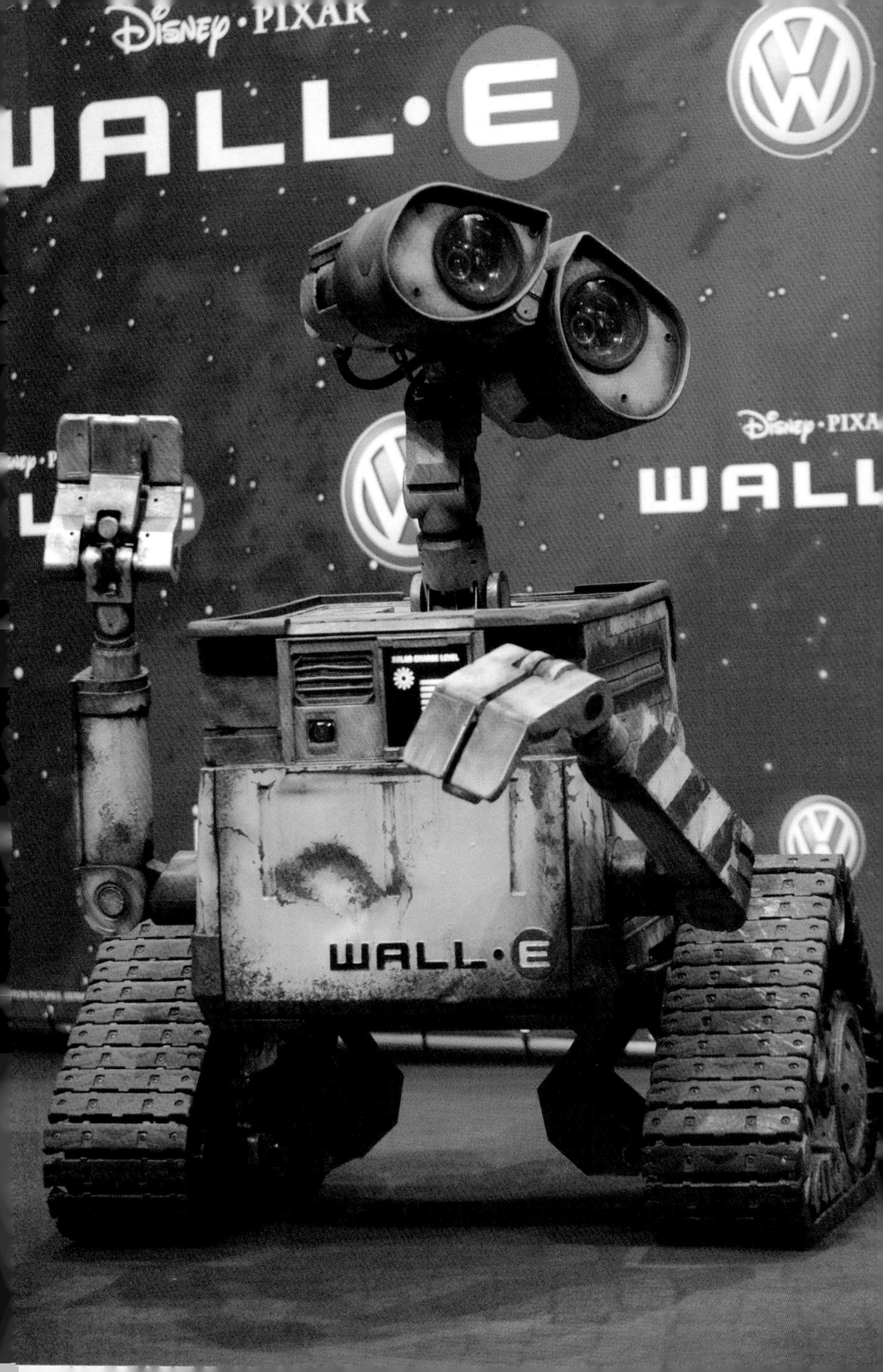
Disney · PIXAR
WALL·E
WALL·E

(2003), *The Incredibles* (2004), *Ratatouille* (2007), and *Wall·E* (2008). These movies from Pixar Studios have been huge box office successes—lots of people have gone to see them and they have made a lot of money. Altogether they have also won twenty Academy Awards.

In 2006 Pixar was sold to Walt Disney Studios. Jobs still works with Walt Disney Studios to make animated movies.

Jobs has been a highly creative person in many fields of technology, including computers, music players, cell phones, and movies.

Steve Jobs is also a family man. He married Laurene Powell in 1991 and they have three children together.

◄ Wall·E at the premiere of the Disney/Pixar movie.

Chapter 7

Apple and Beyond

On December 5, 2007, Steve Jobs received one of many special honors in his life. California Governor Arnold Schwarzenegger and First Lady Maria Shriver inducted Jobs into the California Hall of Fame.

Computers were once thought to be machines that were only useful for work and for business. But thanks to Steve Jobs, they are now used at home, at school, and in almost every part of people's lives. Jobs didn't just change the way we think about computers. He also helped change the way we think about listening to music, thanks to the iPod, and the way we use a cell phone, thanks to the iPhone.

▲ Steve Jobs is congratulated by California's Governor Arnold Schwarzenegger.

He even helped change the way animated movies are made.

Steve Jobs has accomplished so much in his life. No doubt he will continue to develop many more new and innovative products. He truly means what he told the graduating students at Stanford University. "Your time is limited, so don't waste it living someone else's life." That is how he has lived his amazing life so far. What his creative brain will dream up next is certain to be exciting and innovative.

> " . . . have the courage to follow your heart and intuition. They somehow already know what you truly want to become."
> —Steve Jobs

Timeline

1955 Born in San Francisco on February 24

1971 Begins to attend after-school lectures at the Hewlett-Packard Company in Palo Alto; has summer job at Hewlett-Packard and meets Steve Wozniak

1972 Attends Reed College in Portland, Oregon for one semester; drops out of school but still sits in on classes

1974 Returns to California and reconnects with Steve Wozniak

1974 Takes a job at Atari to earn money for trip to India; travels through India studying the people's religious beliefs; returns to USA and goes back to work at Atari

1975 Starts working on a personal computer with Steve Wozniak

1976 Apple I is launched

1977 Apple II goes on sale

1984 Apple Macintosh is created

1985 Leaves Apple for a while and goes to work on other computer ideas

1986 Buys a computer graphics company and renames it Pixar Animation Studios. Pixar begins to make short animated movies.

1991 Marries Laurene Powell

1995 Pixar Animation and Disney Studios make *Toy Story*, the world's first fully computer-animated full-length movie, other fun animated movies follow

1996 Returns to Apple as CEO

2001 iPod is launched

2003 iTunes is launched

2006 Sells Pixar Animation Studios to Disney but continues to be involved with the company

2007 Inducted into California Hall of Fame; iPhone is launched

2008 iPhone and iTouch users download more than 100 million applications from Apple's online App Store

Glossary

animated movies   computer-generated movies that are based on drawings of characters

CEO   the head of a company; CEO stands for Chief Executive Officer

collaborator   someone who works with another person or several people to complete a project

computer graphics   the pictures and letters on a computer screen

investors   people who provide money to help companies get started

innovative   being original or creating something new or different

marketed   sold to different people and businesses

production line   a system for building machines and other things; the machine moves down a line and different people add parts to the machine until it is finished at the end of the line

prototype   first example or model of a product or machine

research   to learn about something; to study or investigate an idea

silcon chip   a small, thin slice of silicon that has a grid of tiny wires built into it with devices that control the way electricity flows through it; used in computers and devices that rely on computer technology

technology   the development of machines that help people work more productively

Learn More

Books

Steve Jobs & Stephen Wozniak: Creating the Apple Computer by K. L. Greenberg (Blackbirch Press, 1994)

Steve Jobs: The Journey is the Reward by J. S. Young (Lynx Books, 1988)

Websites

www.apple.com
www.biography.com/search/article.do?id=9354805
www.pixar.com

Video

Steve Jobs' Stanford Commencement Address:
www.youtube.com/watch?v=UF8uR6Z6KLc

Index